20TH CENTURY DESIGN

DESIGN

THE
60s
THE PLASTIC AGE

For a free color catalog describing Gareth Stevens Publishing's list of high-quality books and multimedia programs, call 1-800-542-2595 (USA) or 1-800-461-9120 (Canada). Gareth Stevens Publishing's Fax: (414) 332-3567.

Library of Congress Cataloging-in-Publication Data available upon request from publisher.
Fax: (414) 332-3567 for the attention of the Publishing Records Department.

ISBN 0-8368-2708-2

This North American edition first published in 2000 by
Gareth Stevens Publishing
A World Almanac Education Group Company
330 West Olive Street, Suite 100
Milwaukee, Wisconsin 53212 USA

Original edition © 1999 by David West Children's Books. First published in Great Britain in 1999 by Heinemann Library, Halley Court, Jordan Hill, Oxford OX2 8EJ, a division of Reed Educational and Professional Publishing Limited. This U.S. edition © 2000 by Gareth Stevens, Inc. Additional end matter © 2000 by Gareth Stevens, Inc.

Editor: Clare Oliver
Picture Research: Brooks Krikler Research

Gareth Stevens Senior Editor: Dorothy L. Gibbs
Gareth Stevens Series Editor: Christy Steele

Photo Credits:
Abbreviations: (t) top, (m) middle, (b) bottom, (l) left, (r) right

Corbis: Cover (ml), pages 8(m), 10-11, 11(t), 17(tl, tr), 20(l), 21(br), 22-23, 23, 24, 25(b), 26(bl), 27(b) / Everett: pages 27(m), 29.
Hulton Getty Collection: Cover (bm), pages 5(m), 6(l, b), 6-7, 14(tl, bl), 15(t, b), 16(b), 18(b), 19(b), 20-21(t), 22(both), 25(t).
MGM (courtesy of the Kobal Collection): page 15(m).
NASA: Cover (bl), pages 4-5, 14(br).
National Museum of Photography Film & Television/SSPL: page 17(b).
Redferns: Cover (tr), page 9(t) / Caroline Greville: Cover (tl), page 9(b).
Irving Solero (courtesy of the Museum at the Fashion Institute of Technology, New York): pages 6(t), 10(br).
Solution Pictures: Cover (br), pages 5(b), 26-27, 28, 28-29(both).
Frank Spooner Pictures: pages 5(t), 8(b), 12(l), 14(t), 24-25, 25(m).
Vitra Design Museum: Cover (m), pages 3, 4, 14-15, 18(t), 19(tr), 20-21(b).
© Vogue/Condé Nast Publications Ltd. / Duffy: page 11(b) / Peter Rand: page 7(br) / Traeger: page 10(l) / Justin de Villeneuve: page 7(bl).
Courtesy of XXO Mobilier et Design, Paris: Cover (tm, mr), pages 19(tl, tm), 20(m, b), 21(mr, bl).

Printed in Mexico

1 2 3 4 5 6 7 8 9 04 03 02 01 00

20TH CENTURY DESIGN

THE 60s

THE PLASTIC AGE

Julia Bigham

Gareth Stevens Publishing
A WORLD ALMANAC EDUCATION GROUP COMPANY

CONTENTS

Plastic was the material of the 1960s. It could be molded into any shape, and it came in vibrant colors. Designers loved it and used it for everything, including fashions, furniture, and tableware.

The United States won the decade-long space race when, in 1969, astronaut Neil Armstrong became the first man on the Moon.

THE FAB 1960s

In this decade of great upheaval, the Cold War between the United States and the Soviet Union over-shadowed the world of politics. Across Europe and the United States, people of different genders and races fought for equal freedoms.

Postwar baby boomers were now young consumers. For most of them, the 1960s were full of optimism and affluence, with plenty of work for everyone. Designers and manufacturers increasingly targeted the baby-boomer market. With full-color illustrations and photographs, magazines promoted a wide range of goods suitable for a trendy young lifestyle, including cars, clothes, and electrical devices.

"Hit parade" shows on TV promoted the music of pop bands.

Both television and films played important roles in popular culture and design. A huge increase in television ownership brought international events, including the Vietnam War, directly into people's homes.

In 1960, John F. Kennedy became the youngest-ever U.S. president. He was assassinated in 1963.

Space mania, fed by the space race, led to TV serials, such as *Star Trek,* and films, such as *2001: A Space Odyssey* and *Barbarella.* The sets and costumes of these productions were on the cutting edge of contemporary design.

With a top speed of 149 miles (240 kilometers) per hour, the E-type Jaguar was the sports car to own.

FASHION

Fashion in the 1960s was one of the most exciting areas of design. The new styles had the look of fun and youth, and, from the miniskirt to the caftan, clothing reflected new freedoms.

This baby-doll minidress (1967) by André Courrèges is pink chiffon with pink satin flowers.

RISING HEMLINES

The most revolutionary look of the decade was the miniskirt, which became a symbol of the liberated 1960s. Although British designer Mary Quant (*b*.1934) has been dubbed "the mother of the miniskirt," others, such as French designer André Courrèges (*b*.1923), also designed shockingly short skirts at about the same time.

MATERIAL WORLD

Many designers experimented with new materials. In France, Daniel Hechter (*b*.1938) made disposable paper dresses, while Paco Rabanne (*b*.1934) worked with plastics, metals, and leather. Dresses and pantsuits, as well as boots, were made out of PVC, a plastic vinyl. American Diana Drew even designed illuminated vinyl clothing — that flashed to the beat of the music!

The pink paisley sleeves of this simple nylon mini-dress (1966) were made to match the tights.

Short hairstyles, such as this bob modeled by Mary Quant, were considered just as shocking as short skirts.

6

HOW ACRYLIC IS MADE

Synthetics first appeared in 1939 but were not widely used until the 1960s. Quick-drying, wrinkle-resistant acrylic was the perfect fabric for young styles. Acrylic was durable, and it took colored dyes very well — for making the swirling paisley patterns of the late 1960s.

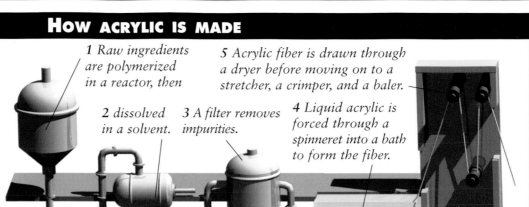

1 Raw ingredients are polymerized in a reactor, then

2 dissolved in a solvent.

3 A filter removes impurities.

4 Liquid acrylic is forced through a spinneret into a bath to form the fiber.

5 Acrylic fiber is drawn through a dryer before moving on to a stretcher, a crimper, and a baler.

"Swinging" London was the 1960s fashion capital of the world. Kings Road and Carnaby Street (left) had many well-known boutiques.

Ethnic clothing, such as this woolen caftan (1967), was popular with both men and women.

THE WORLD MARKETPLACE

Hippie fashions that emerged in the mid 1960s reflected that culture's interests in alternative lifestyles, Eastern religions, and travel. This ethnic-style clothing included Indian fabrics, Native American fringed suede, and Chinese shawls. Influenced by flamboyant pop stars, such as Mick Jagger, men often wore feminine fashions, such as velvet jeans, embroidered or frilled shirts, and silk scarves. Both men and women wore their hair long.

With her wide eyes and pouting mouth, teenage model Twiggy was the face of the 1960s.

POP CULTURE

During the 1960s, young people became more critical of the way the older generation saw the world. Reassessing everything changed, forever, attitudes toward issues of war, gender, color, and class.

PROTEST GRAPHICS

To promote their political views, protesters used graphics, such as posters, badges, T-shirt slogans, and underground magazines. During the Paris riots of 1968, French students produced their own graphics to counter hostile reports issued by the media and the government. The crude style of their cheap linocut images conveyed the urgency of their cause. Similar techniques were used in the United States for Vietnam war protests.

A 1965 protest against the Vietnam War

CRISIS IN CUBA

The Cold War between the United States and the Soviet Union peaked in 1961–1962 with the Cuban Missile Crisis. Even though war was averted, many young people joined the Campaign for Nuclear Disarmament (CND). Disillusioned with those in power, they looked for alternatives. One was the hippie movement, promoting peace and love, which started in San Francisco in the mid 1960s.

Designed in 1958, the CND logo adorned badges and T-shirts.

At Woodstock in 1969, nearly half a million people camped out and listened to top acts, including the Rolling Stones, Janis Joplin, and Jimi Hendrix.

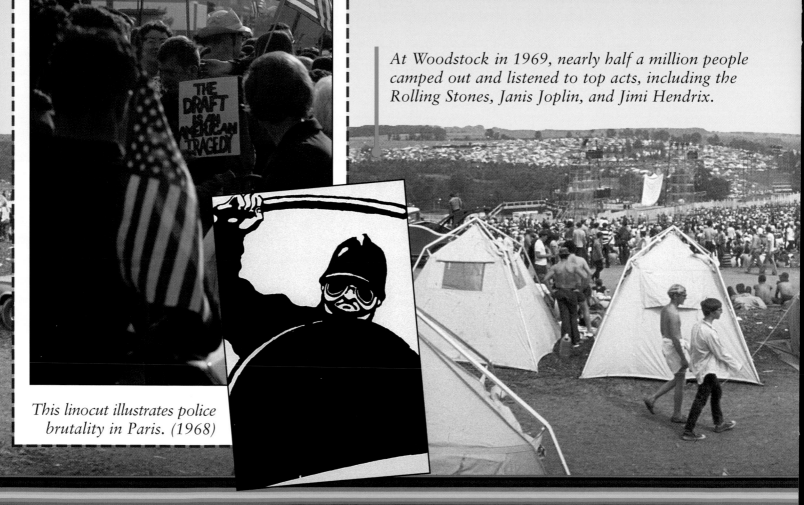

This linocut illustrates police brutality in Paris. (1968)

8

Pop artist Peter Blake and his wife, Jann Haworth, designed the cover for the Beatles' revolutionary Sgt. Pepper *(1967) album.*

The hippies' anti-establishment philosophy of life fostered personal freedom.

POP-STAR POWER

The Beatles were the most successful pop band of the decade, and their "style" had a huge influence on young fans. The group came on the scene with a mod, clean-cut look that included matching suits and neat haircuts. As the decade progressed, however, the Beatles embraced hippie culture. By 1967, when they launched their *Sgt. Pepper* album, they had turned to Indian-inspired music and decadent clothing.

Appropriately, perhaps, the 1960s ended with the biggest rock festival the world had ever seen. At Woodstock in New York State, pop stars and their followers lived out the hippie ideals of peace and love together for one long weekend.

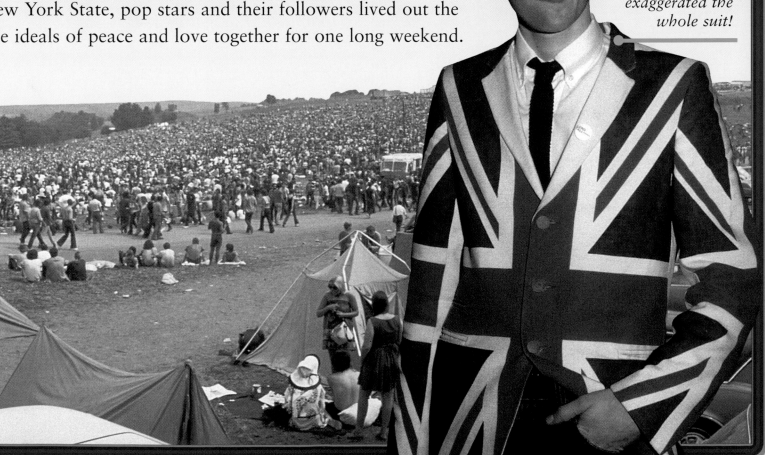

Early mods took a traditional suit and exaggerated the details. Later on, outrageous fabrics exaggerated the whole suit!

9

ART AND DESIGN

The two prominent art styles of the 1960s were pop and op. Pop art was inspired by popular culture, and op art used instantly accessible optical illusions and special effects. Largely because of the nature of these key styles, trends in the art world quickly filtered into mass culture.

With images repeated over and over on it, wallpaper was ideal for pop art. (Warhol's Cow wallpaper, 1966).

The shimmering, moiré-effect velvet of this sun coat, designed by Dutch artist The Fool, created an illusion of movement.

Warhol's "soup" paintings found their way from the art gallery to the catwalk.

EARLY POP ART

Pop art first appeared in the mid 1950s and celebrated the consumerism of popular culture, especially its packaging. British pop art pioneer Richard Hamilton (*b.*1922) used images cut out of magazines for his 1956 collage *Just what is it that makes today's homes so different, so appealing?* The next generation of pop artists included David Hockney (*b.*1937) and Peter Blake (*b.*1932) in Britain and Claes Oldenburg (*b.*1929) and Andy Warhol (1928–1987) in the United States. Warhol captured everything from soup cans to movie stars. His works were silk-screened, not painted, so everything could be endlessly copied, mimicking mass production.

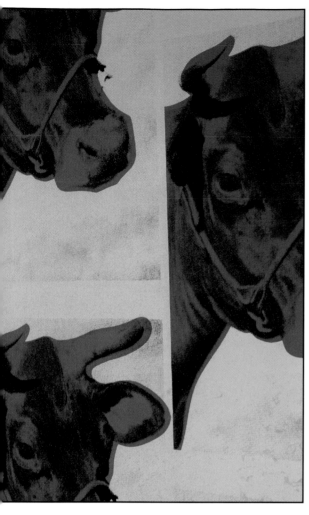

IN BLACK AND WHITE

Op art, short for "optical art," involved the clever use of geometric shapes to create optical illusions. British artist Bridget Riley (*b.*1931) led the way. Initially working only in dramatic black and white, Riley produced dazzling 3-D effects that seemed to move. Op art was widely copied. At the 1968 Olympic Games in Mexico, it inspired everything from the logo to the pavilions.

Op art patterns were perfect for eye-catching fabrics (below left), logos (bottom), posters (right), and the wool trademark (below) designed by Francesco Saroglia in 1966.

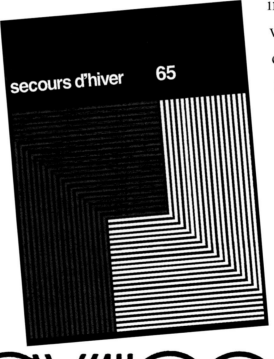

secours d'hiver   65

11

G RAPHICS

As big business and an explosion of entertainment created greater and greater demand for graphic design skills, designers of the 1960s, in growing numbers, were specializing in just one aspect of graphics, such as creating logos or planning advertising campaigns.

This award logo for London's Design Center was introduced in 1959.

Glaring neon often illuminated pop-culture signs, such as this one for the Flamingo Casino in Las Vegas. (1967)

British road signs were given a unified identity in 1964. The color coding and sans-serif typeface followed modernist principles of clean and simple.

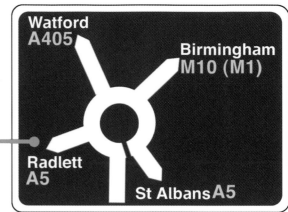

Watford
A405

Birmingham
M10 (M1)

Radlett
A5

St Albans A5

CLEAN AND SIMPLE

The 1950s trend toward clear corporate identities continued into the 1960s. The top graphic designers producing modernist IDs included London-based FHK Henrion (1914–1990), who worked for KLM and BEA airlines, and the American company Chermayeff & Geismar, Inc. (*f.*1960), which redesigned the identities of Mobil Oil and Xerox.

Robert Paganucci updated Paul Rand's classic 1956 IBM logo in the late 1960s.

Tom Geismar's 1964 logo for Mobil Oil used sans-serif type to reduce the letters to simple shapes.

Designer Masaru Katzumie designed simple pictograms for the 1964 Tokyo Olympics.

This logo for Barbara Hulanicki's Biba boutique shows the influence of art nouveau style.

ART NOUVEAU STYLE

In contrast to popular modernist graphics, a trend toward nostalgia and illustration emerged. Logos designed by John McConnell (*b.*1939) for London's Biba boutique used swirling art nouveau lettering that reflected the retro style of the shop's interior and of hippie fashions in general. The Push Pin Studio (*f.*1954), a New York graphic design group, borrowed from Victorian letterforms and Renaissance paintings, combining those elements with witty illustrations.

HIPPIE MESSAGES

As youth rebelled against established society, artists designed posters that promoted underground events and concerts, as well as the general hippie ideals of "Peace" and "Love." Key poster designers included Wes Wilson in San Francisco and Tadanori Yokoo in Japan.

Turn-of-the-century typefaces swirl on these posters by designer Wes Wilson.

13

DEVELOPMENTS IN PRINTING

Phototypesetting, introduced in 1955, sped up printing processes enormously in the 1960s. Hot metal typesetting of the past required assembling a line of words (linotype) or individual letters (monotype) by hand. Phototypesetting used a keyboard to produce light-sensitive sheets of film or photographic paper from which the type could be printed.

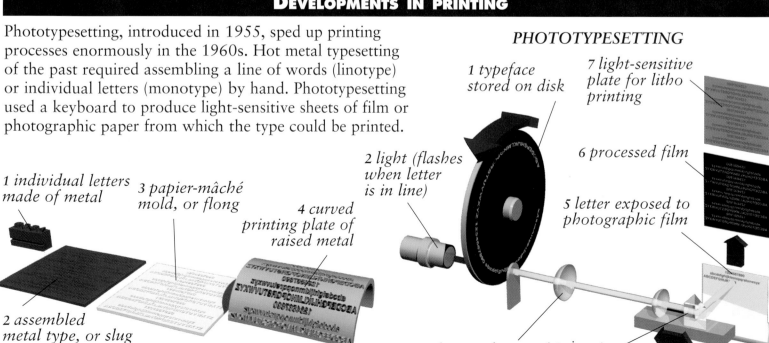

PHOTOTYPESETTING

1 typeface stored on disk

7 light-sensitive plate for litho printing

2 light (flashes when letter is in line)

6 processed film

5 letter exposed to photographic film

1 individual letters made of metal

3 papier-mâché mold, or flong

4 curved printing plate of raised metal

2 assembled metal type, or slug

HOT METAL TYPESETTING

3 lens to focus projected letter

4 prism to bend light

SPACE AGE

The race into space started in 1961 with the Soviet Union's first manned spaceflight. U.S. president John F. Kennedy pledged to put a man on the Moon before the decade was over. On July 16, 1969, the American space-craft *Apollo 11* landed on the Moon.

The 1962 launch of the Telstar *satellite enabled the first transatlantic TV broadcast.*

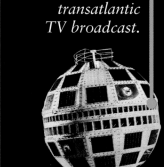

The influence of the Moon landing on design, from interiors to fashions, could be seen at the 1970 Ideal Home Show.

Yuri Gagarin (1934–1968) was the first man in space. In 1961, he orbited the Earth in Vostok 1.

SPACEY REFLECTIONS

Images of rockets, space probes, and satellites had an impact on pop culture, showing up even on textiles and wallpapers, such as the Lunar Rocket wallpaper designed by Eddy Squires in 1969.

FUTURE FASHIONS

Fashions copied space suits! On launching his "Space Age" collection in 1964, Pierre Cardin (*b.* 1922) said, "The clothes that I prefer are those I invent for a life that doesn't exist yet."

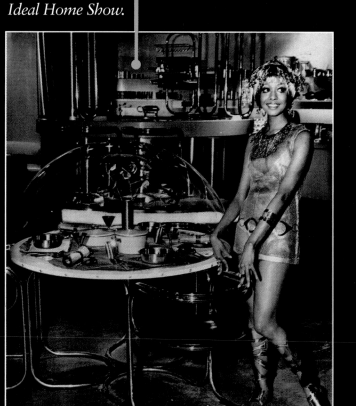

Neil Armstrong (b.1930) was the first man to walk on the Moon.

14

*Models went futuristic —
reflective silver mini-dresses
teamed with glitzy, silver
moon boots — for this
photoshoot on the streets
of Paris in 1969.*

*The 1968 film 2001: A
Space Odyssey influenced
how people imagined life in
space. This attendant on an
interspace station flight is
dressed all in white.*

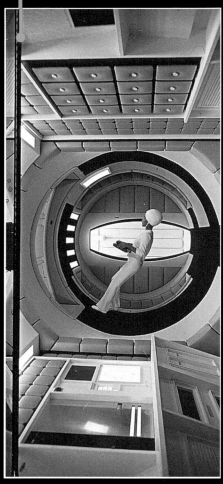

*The Globe Chair (1965), by
Finnish furniture designer
Eero Aarnio, featured
rounded, space-
age shaping.*

FURNITURE OF THE FUTURE

Interior design in the 1960s also
emphasized space-age styles and color
schemes. Walls were often painted white,
and furniture included shiny white PVC
sofas or molded fiberglass creations, such
as those designed by Eero Aarnio (*b*.1932).
Aarnio's creations included the Asko Bubble
Chair and the Globe Chair, both designed in
1965. Even domestic
appliances started
to look like
equipment from
a space station. Television
sets, for example, had curvy styling
and came in brilliant white plastic
casings — a whole new look after
the wood or veneer cabinets that
all televisions had in the 1950s!

*On display in 1961, this "television set of the
future" had white plastic space-age styling.*

GROWING SMALLER

The miniskirt and the Mini car were just two examples of the 1960s trend toward miniaturization. With new technological leaps, such as a growing use of transistors and the invention of the silicon chip (1962), even appliances and electrical devices were getting smaller.

A vacuum holds the heat of the wires inside a valve's glass casing.

A transistor conducts electricity through solid silicon.

Sony's classic transistor radio, the TR610, came in three different colors — red, black, or ivory.

SONY

96

4X4 TRANSISTOR

JAPANESE GIANTS

Although World War II (1939–1945) bombing destroyed almost every factory in Japan, postwar rebuilding gave Japan highly modernized factories.

In the 1950s, Japanese companies, such as Sharp and Sony, became known for electronic goods with lower prices and sophisticated styling, usually black with chrome detailing. Sony also bought a license to manufacture transistors, which were invented in the United States in 1947.

MINIATURIZATION

Transistors meant even smaller appliances. In 1959, Sony's portable TV 80 301 came hot on the heels of its 1958 TR610 pocket radio. The TV won the Gold Award for design at the *Triennale*, a design showcase held every three years in Milan, Italy.

SONY

Sony's Micro TV could run on either electricity or a battery. It put Japan and, particularly, Sony at the forefront of miniaturized design.

VALVES, TRANSISTORS, AND CHIPS

Domestic appliances first used large valves that needed a vacuum to conduct electricity. The transistor, invented in 1947, used silicon and did not need a vacuum, so it could be much smaller. In widespread use by the late 1950s, the transistor paved the way for the silicon chip in 1962. This chip was a tiny circuit board made up of thousands of miniature transistors.

Miniature receiver (1970)

A mini Sony kept some taxi riders amused in 1963. The vehicle's battery powered this tiny set.

TOUCH-TONE PHONES

Bell engineers in the United States revolutionized telephone styling when they invented the Touch-Tone phone in the early 1960s. They arranged numbered push buttons on a grid and gave each column and each row on the grid a unique dial tone. Pressing a button sent a dual, or double, tone to the telephone exchange. One tone revealed the column in which the number appeared on the grid, and the other tone revealed which row. With this information, an operator knew which number had been pressed. This huge advance in telephone technology led to flatter telephones with smaller buttons.

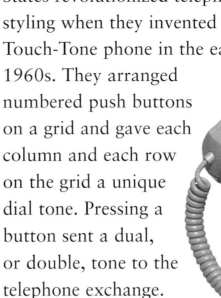

Introduced in 1963, "Touch-Tone" replaced old-fashioned "rotary" dialing.

DESIGN CLASSICS

The trend toward smaller, more compact appliances did not stop with televisions and radios. Combining technology and style, British designer Kenneth Grange (*b.*1929) came up with two of the design classics of the decade, the Kenwood Chef food mixer, in 1960, and the Kodak Instamatic Camera, in 1968. Kodak had asked Grange to design a camera for their convenient new film cartridges.

The Kodak Instamatic Camera, launched in 1968, was simple and compact. Kodak sold more than twenty million Instamatics.

PLASTIC FANTASTIC

The 1960s might be called the Plastic Age. Seen as the material of progress and the future, plastic became popular in both mainstream and alternative cultures. It was inexpensive, disposable, and offered endless design possibilities. Plastic could be hard or flexible, transparent, opaque, or patterned, and could take many different forms.

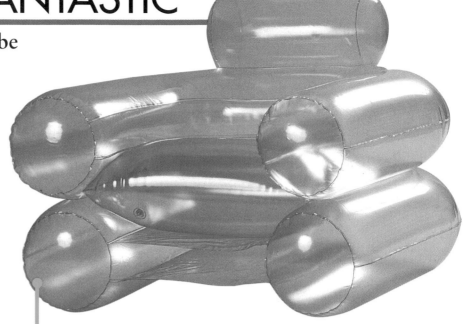

Carlo Scolari, Jonathan De Pas, Donato D'Urbino, and Paolo Lomazzi designed the Blow Chair in 1967. This chair was made of inflatable PVC and came with its own repair kit — for mending punctures.

This transparent TV set has a Perspex casing. It was produced by Sobell in 1960.

SWITCHING TO PLASTIC

In the 1950s, elaborate wood veneers made television sets look like furniture. In the 1960s, designers used molded plastic casings for a high-tech look that reflected the rapid advances in TV technology, such as more channels, better quality programming, and the introduction of color.

ALL BLOWN UP

Plastics suited furniture, too. The Italian firm Zanotta used new welding methods to make inflatable PVC furniture, the first of which was the Blow Chair, in 1967. Other pieces soon followed. Quasar Khan designed sofas and chairs with separate inflatable elements and metal links. Khan's designs could be filled with air, colored gas, or water.

Panton's Globe Light (1970) featured a lightbulb and colored aluminum shades encased in a clear, acrylic globe.

The Stacking Chair, designed by Verner Panton in 1960, went into production in 1967. It was the first one-piece plastic chair.

Quasar Khan designed the Relax Sofa in 1967. Khan was also famous for designing a totally inflatable apartment in 1968 — the walls, chairs, and even the lamps were all blown-up PVC!

PANTON AND PLASTICS

In 1960, Danish designer Verner Panton (1926–1998) created the first all-plastic, injection-molded chair. Panton explored the use of many different plastics, from clear acrylics to polyurethane foam.

19

MAKING PLASTICS

petro-chemicals

heater

hot, liquid plastic inside the reactor

cool water to control the reactor's temperature

extruder

water bath

cutter

hard plastic chip

Plastics are made by mixing petrochemicals with a catalyst to form a polymer. In a large reactor, at an extremely hot 392° Fahrenheit (200° Celsius), the chemicals melt together to make hot, liquid plastic. An extruder feeds the liquid plastic into a water bath, where it cools to form hard, solid plastic. This solid plastic is cut into small chips. Plastic manufacturers can simply melt the chips to mold the plastic.

This model has on a see-through plastic raincoat to show a new see-through plastic phone booth. (1969)

INTERIORS AND FURNITURE

No single style dominated interiors of the 1960s. Scandinavians favored simple designs, usually in natural materials. Radical designers used plastics or enameled metal for their wild creations. Another approach revived the floral designs of times past, and many interiors mixed and matched a variety of styles.

Wicker chairs hang from the ceiling in this 1960s living room.

POP ART SEATING

Inspired by Andy Warhol and Claes Oldenburg, many furniture designers created unusual pieces, which often meant molding materials into pop art-inspired shapes. Leather, for example, was molded into Marilyn Monroe's lips, or vinyl into a baseball glove.

Jonathan De Pas named his 1970 Joe Chair after champion baseball player Joe DiMaggio.

WICKER AND PINE

A revival of art nouveau and Victoriana appeared in the mid 1960s, teaming secondhand furniture with wallpapers that copied the arts and crafts designs of William Morris, for example. Terence Conran's shop, Habitat (f.1964), sold a wide range of household goods, including furniture, kitchen equipment, and bedding. Conran sold wicker chairs and pine tables alongside stackable plastic chairs. Unassembled furniture that could be put together at home was popular, too.

In 1965, French designer Olivier Mourgue created the sculptural Djinn Chair. This molded polyester chair appeared in the film 2001: A Space Odyssey.

Verner Panton and friends try out his new line of plastic chairs in 1964. The chairs could be raised and lowered with cords.

SPECIAL EFFECTS

Experimental interiors became a trend in the 1960s. Some were often disorienting. With their swirling colors and bizarre shapes and images, they could even make a person feel dizzy. Other experimental interiors were designed to be as relaxed and flexible as possible. Verner Panton's avant-garde seating systems, for example, included chairs that hung from the ceiling at adjustable heights, as well as Panton's modular Pantowers — vertical foam columns with various spaces built in for sitting and relaxing.

A furniture store in Copenhagen, Denmark (1960)

This lip-shaped sofa brings to mind Andy Warhol's screenprints of Marilyn Monroe. The sofa is now a museum piece.

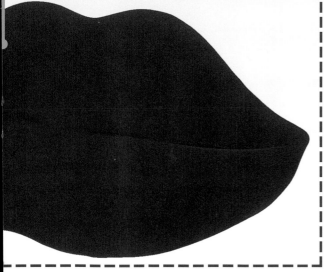

The enameled steel shade of Verner Panton's Flower Pot Lamp (1967) came in different colors.

21

Joe Colombo designed the Universale Chair in 1965. This stackable piece of furniture allowed for more freedom in arranging living spaces.

MODULAR BUILDING

The 1960s saw big changes in the way houses were built. Old-fashioned materials were no longer very popular. Architects wanted to mass-produce houses, making them easier and less expensive to build. Inspired by Le Corbusier (1887–1965), they turned to modular building.

MOVABLE HOUSING

A portable house was the most unusual result of experiments in producing prefabricated homes. A Finnish plastics firm created the UFO-like Futuro, a self-contained, portable house. With its built-in bed, chairs, appliances, and under-floor heating, the Futuro could be moved into almost any landscape.

The Futuro portable house (1969)

POP TOGETHER

Modular building saved a lot of time and money. The parts of a house were prefabricated, or made in a factory, and could be assembled very quickly wherever needed. The parts could be shipped anywhere on Earth, bringing good housing to people who otherwise could not afford it. In theory, modular houses had all the amenities of traditional houses, including modern hygiene and cooking facilities — for a fraction of the price!

OVERNIGHT POD

Habitat '67 was a plug-together apartment complex built for the Montreal World's Fair. Inspired by Japanese capsule hotels, its "module" rooms had space for only one person.

Mass-producing buildings too economically spelled disaster for Ronan Point, a block of British government-built apartments that collapsed after a minor gas explosion in 1968.

Habitat '67 inspired a new vision of home building. While modern architecture tended to be monumental and harsh, Safdie tried to create a mass-produced building with a human scale and surprising variety.

Prefabricated buildings became very popular in the late 1960s. The Constructa 1970 exhibition demonstrated the best of the new construction techniques.

HABITAT FORMING

Habitat '67, designed by Moshe Safdie (b.1938), was the world's first and greatest experiment in modular housing. Modules are made in a series of simple steps that include the installation of kitchens and bathrooms. Cranes hoist finished modules into position, and the modules are anchored with special steel rods. Once builders hook up water and electricity, modules are ready to occupy. Although no modular building is ever really finished (more modules can always be added), Safdie's Habitat has remained the same size since 1967 — just 158 units.

A frame is constructed using steel rods.

Cement is poured over the frame in a wooden mold, or "form," to create a reinforced-concrete module.

Kitchen and bathroom units are put into place.

The finished module is transported to a building site.

GRAND DESIGNS

With the dawn of the 1960s, the dreary task of rebuilding the postwar world ended. Architects were finally free to explore their ideals of designing grand projects for wealthy clients and companies and using the new materials and technologies just becoming available.

NEW FACES

Traditional building methods were abandoned. For example, American architect R. Buckminster Fuller (1895–1983), created the geodesic dome — a structure of geometric faces that distributed the stress of gravity across its surface.

This geodesic dome was built by Buckminster Fuller for the 1967 World's Fair in Montreal, Canada.

24

THOROUGHLY MODERN

Many architects in the 1960s were influenced by Le Corbusier and other modernists, who believed that designers should create a clean, uncluttered living environment. They felt that every building design should be both artwork and a practical tool.

GLASS MASTERED

In the early 1960s, the new float glass process revolutionized glassmaking. Glass floating on molten metal could be formed into perfect sheets. This process saved time and improved quality.

Since architects could now rely on low-cost supplies of large panes of glass, they began to create enormous new skyscrapers with shiny, glass skins.

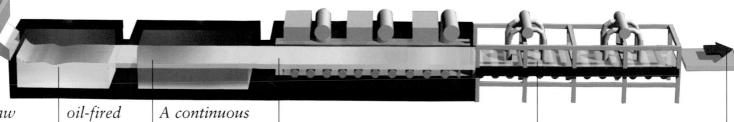

| *raw material mixture* | *oil-fired melting furnace* | *A continuous glass ribbon floats on molten tin.* | *Careful cooling makes the glass ribbon strong.* | *The glass is cut.* | *Glass sheets are shipped to a warehouse.* |

Kenzo Tange used concrete, cables, and steel to create this playful stadium for the 1964 Olympics in Tokyo.

SHOWING OFF

Some extraordinary new buildings were designed for countries that wanted to be seen as leaders in the modern world. The sweeping curves of Tokyo's Olympic Stadium, designed by Kenzo Tange (*b*.1913), showed off Japanese engineering prowess. American architect Minoru Yamasaki (1912–1986) created the New York World Trade Center as a statement of United States economic power. When completed, in 1970, the Center's twin towers were the world's tallest structures.

Each of the World Trade Center's 110-story twin towers has 21,800 windows.

London's Post Office Tower (1964) boldly displays its futuristic gadgetry.

The Metropolitan Cathedral in Brasília.

DESIGN CITY

In 1956, the Brazilian government decided the country needed a new capital city. Oscar Niemeyer (*b*.1907) and his teacher, French-born Lucio Costa (1902–1998), completed the first section of the city in April 1960. They designed the city with separate zones for residents, businesses, government, and leisure. The new capital, named Brasília, featured bold, inspirational architecture. Niemeyer's Metropolitan Cathedral was made of glass shaped like a spiky crown of thorns with a cross "floating" above it.

ON THE ROAD

At the beginning of the decade, the few lucky Europeans who owned cars still had to cope with poor roads. The 1960s boom in car ownership, however, brought new highways with it. These superhighways were a radical new transportation concept that suddenly made traveling long distances by car easy.

MORE — AND FASTER!

Since the 1950s, road traffic had generally increased. The number of cars in London doubled; new *zones bleues* in Paris reduced traffic. New York built urban freeways to handle congestion.

European highways built in the 1960s, however, had no traffic lights or interchanges to slow the flow of vehicles. Furthermore, increased driving speeds made road signs harder to read. So, in 1964, Jock Kinneir (1917–1974) and Margaret Calvert (*b.*1935) redesigned British road signs.

Faster speeds brought new problems for highway designers. Since cars cannot turn tight corners at high speeds, junctions with long, gently curved roads were built.

The 1964 Porsche 911, with its streamlined styling, took the auto-racing world by storm. It won the Monte Carlo Rally in 1968, 1969, and 1970.

Two million Minis had been produced by the end of the decade. The Mini was sporty, inexpensive, and a nice size for young urban drivers.

The 1961 E-type Jaguar inspired a decade of car design. With a top speed of 150 miles (240 km) per hour, it was made for fun.

A CAR FOR PEOPLE

Turkish-born Alec Issigonis (1906–1988), a designer for Morris Motors, believed he could make a popular, long-running car if he avoided strong styling. His 1959 Mini ignored fashionable body shapes, but it was a huge success and stayed in production for thirty years. This 10-foot- (3-meter-) long vehicle relied on a series of amazing innovations to reduce its size.

MADE FOR ROLLIN'

Some people chose life on the road with just a motorcycle. Their unique motorcycles became known as choppers because the bikers "chopped up" old motorcycles for parts to customize them.

Dennis Hopper, Peter Fonda, and Jack Nicholson captured the wild "biker" spirit in their 1969 hit film Easy Rider.

HIPPIE DESIGNS

As the 1960s came to a close, being wealthy and successful became less fashionable. Hippies put spiritual development and psychic discovery ahead of material gains. In conjunction with hippie lifestyles and ideals, vivid and intricate forms of decoration emerged. Elaborate designs were especially popular on cars and buses, where they demonstrated that the owner cared more about creative expression than the resale value of the vehicle.

John Lennon's 1967 Rolls Royce became a collector's item.

HIGH-SPEED TRANSPORTATION

Both business and pleasure travel boomed during the 1960s. The new global companies sent their executives around the world to attend meetings, and families with enough money discovered that a plane ticket to the Mediterranean cost only a little more than a vacation closer to home. To meet these increased travel demands, designers created a whole new generation of public transportation.

In 1969, the Concorde *brought travel time from New York to Europe to within four hours. This supersonic plane can fly as fast as a rifle bullet.*

AS FAST AS A SPEEDING BULLET

Japan influenced the future of transportation in 1964 when it unveiled its super express train, or *Shinkansen*. Sweeping through Japan at speeds of up to 130 miles (210 km) per hour, this "Bullet" train made the world radically rethink its public transportation systems. French and British rapid trains were soon being planned, but short-hop plane flights beat them to the scene.

The Shinkansen, *with its distinctive "bullet" nose, whistles past Mount Fuji.*

MILES ABOVE

Boeing's 707, the first passenger jet in the world, had been redefining air travel since 1958. Then, in 1964, Boeing introduced the 727, a plane with increased capacity that forced countries around the world to enlarge their airports and improve their abilities to handle large numbers of travelers. By the time the 747 jumbo jet arrived, at the end of the 1960s, long-distance travel by air had become quicker and less expensive than any other means of transportation.

AHEAD OF ITS TIME?

Designers must have wondered just how fast they could make a passenger jet fly because, in 1962, Britain and France joined forces to develop a passenger jet that could carry a hundred people and fly at twice the speed of sound. They succeeded, in 1969, with the *Concorde,* but some countries objected to its noise.

In 1969, the Boeing 747 jumbo jet split the cost of a flight between five hundred passengers, making air travel affordable for almost everyone.

James Bond, jet-propelled in a Bell Rocket Belt (1965)

FLIGHTS OF FANCY

Innovations in public transportation during the 1960s made some designers wonder if they could revolutionize private transportation, too. In 1961, the Bell Rocket Belt managed to take off — but it never really caught on! Concepts like the rocket belt, however, led to the creation of leisure planes and hang gliders.

READY, JET SET, GO!

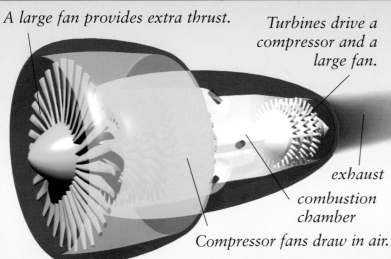

A large fan provides extra thrust.

Turbines drive a compressor and a large fan.

exhaust

combustion chamber

Compressor fans draw in air.

Jet engines invented during World War II to power military planes were extremely noisy and wasted energy stirring up the air behind them without helping to push the plane forward. In 1967, Pratt & Whitney's turbofan engine provided a solution to these problems. An extra turbine at the back turned a big fan at the front, which forced more air through and around the motor, providing extra thrust and reducing the noise. Making less noise meant that jets could land closer to big cities.

· T I M E   L I N E ·

	DESIGN	WORLD EVENTS	TECHNOLOGY	FAMOUS PEOPLE	ART & MEDIA
1960	•*Grange: Kenwood Chef food mixer* •*Panton: Stacking Chair*	•*Belgian Congo granted independence*	•*Laser invented* •*U.S.:* Triton *nuclear sub circumnavigates the world underwater*	•*USSR: Leonid Brezhnev becomes president* •*Madonna born*	•*Yves Klein:* Anthropométries •*Alfred Hitchcock:* Pyscho
1961	•*E-type Jaguar* •*Bell Rocket Belt* •*First* Archigram *magazine*	•*Bay of Pigs invasion of Cuba* •*Berlin wall built* •*OPEC formed*	•*Yuri Gagarin is the first man in space* •*Renault 4 first produced*	•*Ernest Hemingway commits suicide* •*Ballet star Nureyev defects from USSR*	•*Claes Oldenburg opens "The Store," selling plastic replicas of food*
1962	•*Ulm school reworks Lufthansa's identity* •*Giacomo and Castiglioni: Arco lamp*	•*Cuban Missile Crisis* •*Algeria gains independence from France*	•*Telstar satellite launched* •*Silicon breast implant*	•*Marilyn Monroe dies* •*France: Georges Pompidou named Prime Minister*	•*Warhol:* One Hundred Campbell's Soup Cans •*Burgess:* A Clockwork Orange
1963	•*Gropius: Pan-Am Building* •*Quant: Ginger Group* •*Murdoch: Spotty Chair*	•*Nuclear Test Ban Treaty, signed by USSR, UK, and USA*	•*Philips introduces audio cassette tapes*	•*U.S.: President John F. Kennedy assassinated* •*Bruce Reynolds leads Great Train Robbery*	•*Roy Lichtenstein:* Whaam! •*Beach Boys:* Surfin' USA
1964	•*Cardin: Space Age* •*Geismar: Mobil logo* •*Conran opens Habitat* •*Olympic Stadium, Tokyo* •*Biba opens*	•*UN sanctions against South Africa* •*Vietnam War begins* •*PLO formed* •*Olympics, Tokyo*	•*Word processor invented* •*Moog synthesizer invented*	•*Muhammad Ali: world heavyweight champion* •*Mandela jailed in South Africa*	•*The Hollies:* In the Hollies Style •Goldfinger •A Fistful of Dollars
1965	•*Yves Saint Laurent: Mondrian dress* •*Aarnio: Globe Chair* •*Mourgue: Djinn Chair*	•*India and Pakistan at war over Kashmir* •*End of capital punishment in UK*	•*Completion of France–Italy road tunnel through Mt. Blanc*	•*Malcolm X assassinated*	•*Bridget Riley:* Arrest I •Doctor Zhivago •The Sound of Music
1966	•*Warhol: Cow wallpaper* •*Saroglia: wool trademark* •*Seifert: Centre Point, London* •*Magistretti: Chimera Light*	•*Cultural revolution in China*	•*Fuel-injection engines for cars introduced in UK*	•*England's football (soccer) team wins World Cup*	•*David Hemmings:* Blow-Up •*Bob Dylan:* Blonde on Blonde
1967	•*Safdie: Habitat '67* •*Blow Chair* •*Panton: Flower Pot lamp*	•*Six-Day War between Arabs and Israelis*	•*First heart transplant* •*Dolby invents noise reduction system for stereos*	•*Che Guevara killed in Bolivia* •*Artists Gilbert and George first meet*	•*Walt Disney:* Jungle Book •*Beatles:* Sgt. Pepper's Lonely Hearts Club Band •*The Doors:* The Doors
1968	•*Grange: Kodak Instamatic Camera* •*Archigram: Instant City* •*McConnell: Biba logo*	•*USSR invades Czechoslovakia* •*Student riots in Paris* •*Vietnam: Tet Offensive* •*Olympics, Mexico*	•*Aswan Dam completed* •*Collapse at Ronan Point*	•*Martin Luther King, Jr. assassinated* •*Yuri Gagarin dies in plane crash*	•Chitty Chitty Bang Bang •2001: A Space Odyssey •*Marvin Gaye:* I Heard it through the Grapevine
1969	•*Futuro portable home* •*Archizoom: Mies Chair* •*Colombo: Tube Chair* •*Pesce: Up chair series*	•*Stonewall Uprising: beginning of Gay Rights movement*	•*Neil Armstrong: first moon walk* •*Concorde's first flight*	•*John Lennon and Yoko Ono married* •*Ronald and Reggie Kray jailed*	•*U.S.:* Woodstock music festival

GLOSSARY

amenities: features that add comfort, ease, beauty, or charm to either a place or a social situation.

caftan: a loose-fitting, ankle-length garment, of Mediterranean origin, that usually has long, full sleeves, is made of cotton or silk, and is sometimes cinched at the waist.

consumerism: the practice of catering to, or even exploiting, consumer interests for the purpose of increasing product purchases.

extruder: an auger-style tool used to push, press, or otherwise force material, such as metal or plastic, through a shaping device known as a die.

flong: a papier mâché material used to make molds that hold metal type in place for printing.

hippies: individuals whose appearance and lifestyle reject the conventions of established society and promote nonviolence.

linocut: the print of a design that has been cut into a piece of linoleum.

litho: short for "lithograph," which is printed material produced through lithography, a process that transfers images from a flat surface by holding ink on image areas but repelling ink from non-image areas.

moiré: a wavy or ripplelike finish on a fabric that gives the material a watered appearance.

paisley: a patterned fabric, originally made in Scotland of soft wool, marked with a characteristic design of colorful, swirling, abstract and floral-like figures.

polymer: a compound formed by the chemical reaction of two or more elements combining to create a larger molecule of the same elements but with different physical properties.

PVC: the abbreviation for "polyvinyl chloride," which is a synthetic plastic material.

MORE BOOKS TO READ

The 60s: Mods & Hippies. 20th Century Fashion (series). Kitty Powe-Temperley (Gareth Stevens)

The 1960s. A Cultural History of the United States Through the Decades (series). Gini Holland (Lucent Books)

Airlines of the 1960s. Gerry Manning (Motorbooks International)

Bikes, Cars, Trucks, and Trains. Voyages of Discovery (series). Gallimard Jeunesse (Scholastic)

Interior Solutions from Armstrong: The 1960s. C. Eugene Moore (Schiffer Publishing, Ltd.)

Moshe Safdie. Wendy Kohn, *et al*, editors (John Wiley & Son, Ltd.)

Plastics: Molding the Past, Shaping the Future. Encyclopedia of Discovery and Inventions (series). Judith C. Galas (Lucent Books)

Pop Art. Art Revolutions (series). Linda Bolton (Peter Bedrick Books)

Terence Conran: Design and the Quality of Life. Elizabeth Wilhide (Watson-Guptill)

Zenith Transistor Radios: Evolution of a Classic. Norman R. Smith (Schiffer Publishing, Ltd.)

WEB SITES

PFG: The History of Glass. *www.pfg.co.za/history.htm*

Sandretto Plastics Museum. *www.sandretto.it/museonew/UKmuseo*

Sixties Central. *www.geocities.com/FashionAvenue/Catwalk/1038/contents.html*

Tadanori Yokoo. *www.meyercom.com/public/art/yokoo.htm*

Due to the dynamic nature of the Internet, some web sites stay current longer than others. To find additional web sites, use a reliable search engine with one or more of the following keywords: *acrylic, architecture, Boeing, bullet train, Concorde, fashion, furniture, glass, hippie culture, Mini car, op art, plastic, pop art, Mary Quant,* and *Andy Warhol.*

INDEX